STARLIGHT ON WATER

Tessa —
with very best wishes

HELENA NELSON

STARLIGHT ON WATER

Helena Nelson

fife 2003

A _{THE}RIALTO
First Edition

First published in 2003 by
The Rialto
PO Box 309 Aylsham Norwich
England NR1 6LN

First Edition of 500 copies
Typeset in Perpetua 11 on 12.5pt
Design by Starfish, Norwich
Printed by Printing Services (Norwich) Limited

ISBN 09527444-5-7
The publisher acknowledges financial assistance from the Arts
Council of England and East England Arts.

The Rialto is a Registered Charity No. 297553

ACKNOWLEDGEMENTS

Acknowledgements are due to the editors of the following magazines, who first published some of these poems: *Ambit, Deliberately Thirsty, Frogmore Papers, Magma, Obsessed with Pipework, Other Poetry, Poetry Nottingham International, Riverrun, Seam, Snakeskin, The Dark Horse, The Formalist, The Interpreter's House, The Rialto, Weyfarers*.

Two poems also appeared in Forward Collections, and poems from the Mr and Mrs Philpott series appeared in pamphlet form as *Mr and Mrs Philpott On Holiday At Auchterawe & Other Poems*.

CONTENTS

RELEASE

A delicate tampering up on the roof.
It is me. I am easing the parchment of slate.
I have filled your satellite dish with pearls.

Free—I am free. Out at last.
I have come to console, to assert, to assuage.
I am sliding my skin right over your house.

Listen to me. I am the drummer.
I was invited to play. I am clean.
Let me in, let me in. I can permit

anything. Even the sky admits me.
Fingers drop in your mouth. Confess.
Open your body. It beats like a door.

DREAD

Dread, or something like it,
took my hand.
Love is the great destroyer, it said.
You should understand.

If I loved, I would
understand, I said.
But a voice from childhood
is in my head.

It says love is pure
and good and kind
and brings heart's ease
to a troubled mind.

Yes—in the early stage,
said Dread,
—but destruction follows
on love's light tread

wiping out comfort
with its black glove
and seizing everything
else but love

and dread. You'll have me
in your home, in your bed.
Ah—if I loved,
I'd have you, I said.

COLDSTREAM COTTAGE, ARDNAMURCHAN

It's a small white house beside the sea
where the hills are steep and the sky is low
and sheep meander from scree to scree
and sometimes you see a fishing boat go.

The yellow lamplight welcomes you
to a seat by a fire that warms and glows.
An ill wind flusters outside, it's true
but it's calm inside as the darkness grows.

You say, *There's nothing to fear tonight,*
I can rest in peace. If it were so
a haven might mean the world was right.
The floorboards creak and the curtains blow.

Sleep meanders from scree to scree
and the hills are dark and the moon is low.
You hear the snuffling of unease
on the stones, by the door, at the back window.

You toss in a sea of quilted dread
as the black mouth opens, long and slow
and swallows you in your safe white bed
dreaming. You are the last to know.

SNAKE

It was part of the vow we kept
that your pet snake should lie in the bed.
Sounds far-fetched, I know. And snakes are phallic.
But this one was tame, pure black and very shy,
a neat dark coil with quietly golden eyes.
The king-sized bed had space for three of us.
Love slept.

At first there was nothing to confide
the shrinking was so imperceptible.
We lay quite close, each other's next of skin,
and rarely gave much thought to the pet snake
nuzzling nearby. Our dreams stretched
as the marriage bed grew small.
Love sighed.

The problem was the snake, an adept
consumer with voracious appetite.
Mere food was not enough to meet its needs
or slake its hunger; it began to maul
the mattress. Bit by bit, it was eating the bed.
It didn't, somehow, interrupt our rest.
Love wept.

Soon there was no room for you at all. The snake
curled closer to my head. As I said,
part of the deal. I didn't think it dangerous
of course—it was now my pet, not yours.
So you moved out of the bed and onto the floor.
Suddenly the creature stirred and spoke.
Love woke.

I blamed the reptile. 'It's got to go,'
I said. 'Honestly—it's eaten our whole bed.'
'For God's sake,' you replied, 'look quick at the pillow
where the thing sleeps.' I looked, looked again—
the snake was gone. 'Who ate the mattress then?'
I cried. 'And what did the snake say?'
Love's dead, it said.

IRONING DAY

I've never had an ironing board cover that fits
or a baby of my own.
None of the doors here properly shuts
and the garden wall's come down.

But I shouldn't ever want to lose my iron.
Pressing hard, I remember
grass between my toes
and the soft rain of September.

LATE-IN-SEPTEMBER AFTERNOONS

Into some silence rich like jam
preserved and sealed I am,
fixed in sweet transparency
where fruit drinks syrup sea by sea,
lost in sunlight, burnt as old
as carapace of marigold.
Here your words will melt as slow
as summer, love, or snow on snow.

TRAVELLER

Floating from nowhere
into somewhere
into air,
he grabs a balloon
which is air also, air with a skin,
and to this he attaches a wicker basket.

The basket is a shopping basket
and soon it is filled with objects and people
and money and cars
and the weight bears him down,
down to the ground.
Quickly he chucks out
all the spare beds,
two cans of weed-killer, three old friends.

Up he goes, *up*.
A fine view from a fine basket.
This is the life. Everything else
stays in beside him
unless it's exchanged for something better,
lighter, finer.

And then one day
for no earthly reason
he topples out even his last possessions,
flings them all out. Strings in one hand,
he severs the basket

and soars out of sight.
No idea where the air will take him
or how long he'll hold,
hold on, hold on
to all he has left. His voice
floats back. *Love*, it says,
love....

ILLUMINATION

You are not beautiful, or tall,
or very dark, or very fair.
In a crowd, I might not notice you—
your ordinary clothes and hair.

You're self-contained. You remind me of
a light in a box with the lid held shut.
I wonder what I would find inside
if I opened it, if I ventured—but

this is my secret. Locked away
I keep you where my heart stands still,
where darkness covers, and my mouth
is silent as a stone until

you charge me with your honest eyes,
like questions beautiful and plain.
I shall not try to speak, I think,
and hesitate and pause—and then

shocked by an unexpectedness
I did not think to call my own,
I find my heart has turned again
into the sun, the sun, the sun.

BIKE WITH NO HANDS

One look at you and I knew
you'd be able to ride a bike with no hands.

I tried it, of course, but could never do it.
It was written all over your face that you
would have practised, bare legs, bloody knees,
in the Summer evenings, hours at a time
when no-one was watching the mishaps, until
casually, coolly, at infinite ease,
you'd ride, no-handed, surveying the street,
as if you'd been born on a circus bike.

I wish— But then, we are what we are.
I drive with two hands, walk with both feet
firmly planted on sensible ground. And
I've got you. Who can ride with no hands.

FLOWERS

The affair was all coming and going
in snatched half-hours.
Not seeing the need
he never brought flowers.

Bring me a plant,
I asked — a forget-me-not
out of your garden.
He forgot

and came empty-handed,
sorry, blue-eyed.
I don't need flowers,
I said (lied).

He was always leaving.
Once he gave me his cold.
I cherished it, wishing
I had him to hold.

On balance, though
one thing was good:
he told me the truth.
I knew where I stood.

In my green courtyard
for hours, days, years
I stood where I knew,
waiting for flowers.

ULTIMATUM

Easter then, I said.
Is that an ultimatum? you replied.
You could call it that, I thought,
shivering into absurd
dread at the ill-wrought
darkness of last words.

Easter came and went.
Then it was May, and June.
You're out of time, I said,
shivering in my room
at the slow tread
of quick-stepped doom.

So is it now? you asked.
Is the ultimatum now?
Yes it must be, I thought,
shivering in the cold
embrace you taught
my empty house to hold.

I touched your mouth
trembling the words
and your empty hands
shivering, your head bent
to the lonely lands
that Summer meant

and I leaned and tasted
your skin. Ah, your skin.
Come to bed, I said
shivering, *now*. Time later
when sad love's fed
to talk ultimata.

THE INVISIBLE MAN

It must have been the power of his voice
that drew my body to his naked self.
So naked he that nobody could see
his skin as thin as daylight, and his hair
as soft as evening, clear as air.

My tips of fingers sensed his heartbeat
just. I heard more than I felt.
I lay in bed beside a curve of space
and wished for an arm's weight,
or a mouth, or a breath upon my breast.

Not what I got. No—he was invisible.
Invisible, but certainly quite real.
He won my heart with words that caught my soul.
I ached to feel the tangents of his voice,
the arc of words, the movement always *in*.

I fell so far that balance was quite gone
as any fool could see. Witness the vivid way
a wall of mirrors glittered back my flesh, while he
stood emptily beside me, weightless, faint.
Even the carpet pile was scarcely moved.

I asked a friend to tell me what she thought.
She said that love was hard at the best of times
and then complained of much that grieved her eyes.
Oh, but I couldn't see him to lament
his dirty shoes, his towels left on the floor

and couldn't make him visible
no matter how I tried. Love can't unmagic magic
or see things turn out right. Quite the reverse.
'Don't speak to me. It may be easier,' I said.
'Speak only if you've found a way to be

that I can live with.' (He knew I meant 'see'.)
Since then I haven't heard.
Daily I fade, plead to the mirrored wall:
Who is the most invisible of all?
I hope it'll be quick. The silence is terrible.

PLIERS

Heavy, symmetrical, cold and firm,
You grip my grip with unsevered calm,
Locking your jaws in a silent line.

If I squeeze— if you choose— wires will snap.
I hold your potency snugly weighed;
Your curious heels confirm my palm.

Tool that enlarges rule of thumb—
Man in his eager, fierce intent
Has made you do what you would not do—

Your cutting edge betrays the harm.
Forceful friend, unforced for me
Curve in my careful touch, grow warm.

Light reflects on your angled head,
Your metal planes, your steely press.
Hush. My hand engages your arms

In confidence. The nubs of your limbs
Tease my fingers, plead with my skin.
You open as smooth as a pirouette.

METHOD

Memories seethe in the pit,
hissing. Don't worry—
I am training them.
I sing three notes, true and pure.
They hear—and one rises up.
I peg it neatly by the neck,
sad old sock.

The next thinks he will strike
but wait little snake
little old snake—
I have the charm, I can make
viper slow
into slow slow worm.
My voice is warm.

Now the writhing is almost nice.
Once I misjudged: a green vice
narrowed my veins.

Practice, practice. Perfect pitch.
Inconstant slitherers scrape and scratch,
ease off their skins, green to blue.
A sly disguise. One to watch.

Three notes, pure and true.
Were it not for you, I should not sing.
I should not sing, were it not for you.

IMPEDIMENTS

Believing it would stay the same,
  from circumstance apart,
I banished all concern for my
  unalterable heart.

I moved away, my small effects
  in packages arranged.
I did not contemplate my heart
  or find its essence changed

but had I somehow guessed the truth,
  I would not—still—have faltered,
no longer thinking love as true,
  unalterably altered.

'DESERVE HAS NOTHING TO DO WITH IT....' *

get what you deserve?
no
you get what you get

you wash you cook you supplicate
you fold you starch you preen you prink
you get what you get

you serve you kneel you lick the shoes
you fawn you coax you bake new cakes
and get what you get

what you get is coming for you
what you get's unerring
what you get's bespoke and sheer
and ready for wearing

you clean the stairs you moisturise
you shake you press you undertake
and not what you deserve you get
not what you have earned you get
not what you desire you get
but what you get you get

no point trying to escape
the fact (albeit upsetting)
that what you have deserved has swerved
and this is what you're getting

just desserts are what you don't
get—not all not any
hurts it hurts it hurts it hurts

no use
whining

* *A line spoken by Clint Eastwood in the film 'Unforgiven'.*

GENDERALISATION

Women keep scales in their bedrooms;
   men keep weights.
Women eat flaky pastries and sticky toffee pudding with cream;
   men eat steaks.

Women worry about breasts, buttocks and cellulite on thighs;
   men watch them.
Women read about colourful new ways of preparing fish;
   men catch them.

Women go shopping for pleasure;
   men don't.
Women do their best to ignore cricket, golf, snooker and football;
   men won't.

Women are emotional and prone to flights of excess;
   men are self-contained.
Women go to the toilet together in pubs;
   men refrain.

Women write poetry straight from the heart;
   men from the head.
Women like to recline on the grass in the sun;
   men in bed.

Women write a thousand Christmas Cards
   for men to post.
Women prepare turkey, gravy, bread sauce, stuffing, sprouts, roast
   potatoes, mashed potatoes, roast parsnips, sausages wrapped in
   bacon, cranberry sauce, julienne carrots and peas;
   men make toast.

Women launch into long generalisations about men and women;
   men say, "You'll
come across exceptions."
   Which proves the rule.

THE PROFESSIONAL ENGINEER-POET

Though lime does not become him
the professional engineer-poet
cultivates light of that colour
in which to disengage his famous couplets.

Articulation, to the engineer-poet,
is archaic, for he erects
girders which suspend incredible ideas:
nobody knows how they stay up.

He has dispensed with the ingenuity
of rhythmic links in favour of happenstance;
he manufactures what would appear to be prose
were it not for the subtle nuance
of utmost pause and invisible welding.

Longevity is his hallmark. He can suspend
his thought over page on page,
sometimes deliberately leaving one blank
reminder of artifice. Witty extrusions arrest
insightful travellers and rare-word collectors.
Synaptical, cornucopeic and mirabolantic, oho.

He opens the umbrella universe,
impresses while leaving no impression
and reigns.

FROM 'INTERROGATING THE SILENCE'

I

I haven't forgotten looking forward
to seeing you, looking through the warm air
and sun into the lane; and how you moved
slowly towards me, you'd come, you were there,
your tense mouth ready for anything, your
eyes on the horizon and then on me.
And how I coloured, knowing we both shared
the same purpose and that it would all be
purposeful. The meniscus. The bright brink.
Like filling a bowl with water so full
that I could hardly carry it, so full
that nothing could ever be added, all
life and breath steady and clear in the bowl,
all I would ever need to eat or drink.

II

After all, we were true to one another
if not to anybody else. We knew
something imperishable, something neither
of us betrayed. The tide was high when you
put your arms around me. I opened out
my secret self—everything unfastened
slowly. Time waited. Look, *look* at it—
I talk and cry. You hold me and listen.
That moment must be true to itself, true
to its own present. How else can we make
sense of inconsistency? What happens
must happen, just as one event leads to
another. Each tiny wave has to take
its faithful place. Ebb and flow. Consequence.

III

Blowing a kiss to his green-eyed mistress
he prepares himself. Confident, they stand
facing each other. She smiles. No distress
as he twirls his moustache, flicks one hand and
hurls a knife at her heart. *Ah*—the crowd gasps.
She only laughs, her breasts swelling serene
beneath her bodice. Suddenly he clasps
a second blade. It turns in the light, keen
to pierce its soul into the spinning wheel
on which she now revolves, her eyes aglow
with his sharp love, embracing her in steel
like her life's truth. The highlight of the show
illumines all. The knives are meant to *miss*.
I love you—but—you need to practise this.

IV

Your letters matter more than you will know.
You write; I keep them one by one, as snug
as acorns in their shells. I go to them
if all else fails. When the north-east wind blows
and tugs at the curtains, when my heart has dug
a hole for itself, when nothing can stem
obliteration—no place else to go—
I open them. Each word's familiar
and new. Curious. I'd forgotten how
simple handwriting, the touch of your pen,
could bring me almost instantly to where
I'm myself again. Useless to pretend
I understand my own analysis.
Sometimes, though, the letters are all there is.

V

On one of the very bad days, I cried
in a new way, in a way I didn't
cry when you were there—but this time I did—
and there was nothing to say. I couldn't
watch you go again. I had to get out.
There was a picture I liked, a ploughed field
with a farmhouse and some trees. They were shut
safe and sound in their Rowland Hilder world
until I stepped in and entered a place
where reality had been rearranged.
I found the holidays we hadn't had
and the children. A plate of bread and cheese.
My husband. Quietness. The table laid.
And the crying had stopped. Something had changed.

VI

You've never seen my jealousy set loose
because I keep her chained. The place she sleeps
is deep and stone and chill. A brazen noose
encircles her hot throat—mostly it keeps
her teeth at bay. A daily douse of ice
prevents her blood from boiling. But her eyes
terrify most. They bleed with avarice.
She wants and wants and wants. No compromise.
She waits with deadly patience, knowing she
outlives most men. Her red hair seethes and glows,
filling the air with snakes. Resentfully
she squats and broods. Occasionally she grows.
No pet. You can neither tame nor breed her
and it isn't wise to—no—don't feed her.

VII

Love is inhabited by cruelty.
It can strip gentle skin to the quick, tear
flesh to ribbons. It has no sympathy.
It doesn't stop to think. It doesn't care.
No matter how gentle two lovers are
they will be vile. They are secretly hard.
They have gone into a dimension where
the things that matter have all disappeared.
Whatever they say—whatever they write—
they are okay. Hot perhaps, but then cool.
Fair play is exchanged for unfair delight.
They don't want to be nice. They like it cruel.
Racked and trembling, pale victims of lust,
their paroxysms mimic self-disgust.

VIII

The sheets are white. The bed is washed and clean.
The air is light. The heart's sand-papered smooth.
The walls are high, the window-space serene.
Absence insists. No pulse, no voice, no breath.
Dust-flowers tumble freely. Something deepens.
Loose papers flutter. Fluff affects the floor.
A door uncloses slightly and opens
silence

IX

You called me Marco Polo, and I laughed.
I didn't know where I was going.
I hadn't got a map, just the first draft
of a poem. You were in it, knowing
nothing of the bridge that had to be crossed.
Or maybe you did. It's hard to be sure.
One or other of us—or both—had lost
a sense of direction. Not any more.
That's the way it goes. You can't always see
how the path dwindles at the journey's end
though you think you can. Listen to me:
Other fish in the sea. What goes around
comes around. It was never meant to be.
The road to hell is paved with clichés, friend.

X

Often it wasn't unlike attempting
that fairground game—a handful of ping-pong
balls and dozens of glass bowls, opening
false mouths. Every last throw would bounce wrong,
merrily dancing anywhere but in—
and that gaudy music playing. I'd spend
everything I had and more. I would win
nothing. Not one tiny fish. When my hand
was finally exhausted from throwing
I'd come home alone to my quiet house
without you—my unattainable prize.
It was a crazy thing to do. Going
to the fair is a waste of life. What use
is a goldfish? You get it home. It dies.

XI

Stuck in stupid sonnets. Bloody silly
overture to life. Another constraint,
another painful replay of will-he/
won't-he long after the terminal *won't*.
It's self-indulgent—this not letting go—
imposing the frame on each naked fact.
The last time I saw you, caught in a queue
in the driver's seat, you hid your face—act
of a desperate man. It was too much.
After a certain point, nobody wants
to prolong the thing. Or read about it.
Time to stop. What a catalogue—oh such
an unending list of dreary complaints.
And if you think it's finished, forget it.

XII

I'd never wanted to be beautiful
so much as then. I wanted you to fall
without a moment's hesitation, all
of you heart-stopped by my face and your whole
world secondary to my loveliness.
In my imagination I was tall
and willowy. I was off to the ball
with emerald eyes and slippers of glass.
How silly I was. They vanished—the dress
and the beauty. You waited in the rain
until midday. Later I ran away
and shrank, like washing, into littleness.
I am Mrs Tiggywinkle again,
scuttling up the hill with my irony.

THE ONLY EXPLANATION

We are dying, dying—now.
Crushed by kisses, lovers
have the privilege of knowing
what only love discovers:

that life, life is going
and there will be no survivors;
neither passion's pain nor promises
can intercede or revive us

so lovers grab love quickly—
there isn't time to pretend
that life, love, is forever
and the end isn't the end.

MIRROR THEORY

I

I know, I know.
Life is a pool of mirrors
through which you wade for miles
to find your true reflection

and at last, at last
you recognise yourself:
the mean, the cruel,
the spiteful little body.

Yes, yes. You saw her
in my eyes at first,
these little lakes,
these flooded halls

of truth, and truth to tell
I mirror you most faithfully.
like an expected mother.
But I am not your mother.

II

There's no need to
● give up smoking
● get bigger breasts

Show him a reflection
of the man he really wants.

Mostly it's easy. He wishes to be
● tall and resourceful
● desirable and potent

Lift up the heavy glass. See?
He falls in love with himself
and you can have him, little Echo,
so long as you can bear the weight.

But put down the mirror, even for a moment,
and someone else may pass
with another glass.

LITTLE MISS SMART ARSE

You never said it but I saw you think
Little Miss Smart Arse a hundred times.
I took you places, picked you up,
gave you presents on your birthday,
tried so hard. Little Miss Smart Arse.

You made us laugh. You were so funny:
excoriating. I wept with laughter, wished
you would like me, offered more gifts,
talked too much, drove right to your door
but not in. When you left I was sorry.

I wanted to tell you, quickly, quickly,
something unclever, something to show you
we could have been friends
if your mouth hadn't said, "Cheerio. Merry Christmas"
just as my head mouthed— *Little Miss Smart Arse.*

THE SHADES

On the pillow, alive, his breathing Head.
Outside, the whispering waiting Dead.

On the journey to Bone, he is half gone
And their numbers have grown.

A breath. A blink. Grain by grain
time sculls in the burning brain.

It is slow. It is long and slow and late.
They cluster. They wait.

THEN

I will be small. I will be small as
the small flowers of gypsophila—no—
small as a pixel, small as
a small (the smallest) thought you had
last Saturday at five past two.
Small as a light a million miles away; small
as a deaf sound, as a dumb tune, small
as the unmade.

And close. Closer than them all.

AFTER THE NINTH

I was the cat next door come back from the dead.
That paving slab could not keep me down. I clawed
my way through earth and solid stone and flew
at the window. They were inside—the foolish woman
half-weeping, my sleek sister curled asleep
on the man's knee. I freaked. The night fractured
in great cracks. They did not admit me. They—
who had shut me in every night—*watched the TV*.
Enraged, I went to the death car, slivered in
and left a turd on the driver's seat, freshly
mildewed; on the headlamp glass I smeared new blood.
I shall avenge myself while my silver sibling
wastes her lives. I'll pounce on feeble dreams
as they flutter like bats. I'll crush them, devour them whole.

MENS SANA IN CORPORE BANANO

My mother read bananas make you calmer.
I was impressed. I flew out to Havana
and purchased fifty sacks of best banana
from Mario Pax, a small banana farmer.
I hurried home, convinced the gift would calm her
but mother simply snarled. I got my armour
and put on metal gloves—oh not to harm her—
but just to help me force the first banana
between her fangs. It did, I think, disarm her.
She ate ten more. And then some ham from Parma
looking quite pleased. Desperate to charm her
I offered yet another ten bananas.
At last it seemed no gesture could alarm her—
she scoffed the lot, as reverent as a palmer
or teenager spaced out on marihuana,
then wolfed tabasco sauce and pickled llama
with marmalade and lashings of piranha.
At last she smiled and with one cry—*Nirvana!*—
she dropped down dead. O mater, mater alma!
Your visage grim has never been much calmer
and never will again. The nice embalmer
(his name was Vasco, like the great da Gama)
observed that *he* was partial to banana.
He looked on sudden death as simply Karma,
a fitting end to every mellow drama.

THE RAVELL'D SLEEVE OF MA

It wasn't just a hobby. Herbert's Mum
knitted him woolly sweaters by the score.
Give us a hug, Ma, infant Herbert begged
before another jumper (acid green)
shut him up with wool dragged over his eyes.
At eighty-four the ageing matron died,
leaving her grown-up son some minor bills
and ninety-seven sweaters, scarcely worn.
A loose thread started him: one little pull
and off he went—*un*knitting jumpers—winding
up his grief like a man possessed. Then as
the house filled up with wool re-skeined
he broke into a song—just like his mum
when casting on. Renouncing golf and squash
and stamp-collecting too, he wound bright globes
around and round and round and heaped them up
each evening in the hall. He'd always thought
his mother's love was strange; at last he saw,
inspecting his collection (no mean pile),
she'd given him her all, and all was balls.

INSIDE HIS HOUSE SHE BUILT HER HOUSE OF WORDS

At first it was very tall and thin—
she could hardly get in.
She dismantled the upper storeys,
extended the kitchen, widened the doorways.
Still there were too many apologies;
she wanted permissions
and colour. She made the house
talk to itself—a million echoes.
Photographs were to be expected
but not the mirrors reflecting
endlessly and corridors
and fireplaces and secret stairs.
Under the skylight, there was a piano
and geraniums at every window.
There were rooms for writing, sleeping, thinking
and a library linked to
an ironing room whose sheets of light
fluttered with lavender and violet.
On the roof a pool of summer rain
ushered a sudden garden
full of butterflies and birds—
all of them made out of beautiful words.

THE LATE MUSE

She was at it again. Two a.m.
and her nagging would not stop:
Do it like this, and this. No, *this*.
I couldn't sate her;
she would not lie down.

There was very little choice:
I sharpened my arrow to a point
and sent her to oblivion.
No more harping on and on and on.
Not one command. Gone.

I sleep so well with her dead,
so well. No-one to tell me
how to be immortal, no-one to interrupt
my unannounced tranquillity
with trivial recollections.

I have had some hard words set in lead
where the late Muse is interred:
May Her Bones Rot.
We'll see what mice come out to play
with the bitch away—

COMPLETING THE OUTFIT

I used to wish you'd put your hands just so
about my waist, spanning me here and here,
encircling me in love and trust, although
you never knew I cherished the idea.
A small thing. Doesn't matter. Time is gone.
Your hands, so square and kind, don't speak to me.
My waist has come to terms with life alone.
My breathing's calm. My heart goes quietly.
I find these days I like to wear a belt.
I bear it like your touch around the core.
It keeps me safe. Quite recently I felt
I had to tighten it. I think it's more
than reassurance in well-seasoned leather:
it may be all that's holding me together.

DISTANCE

I can see a thin, grey, old woman
behind my beautiful daughter
who is thousands of miles away
across much deep water

and my beautiful daughter is laughing—
she doesn't see the old woman with nails like claws
but the old woman sees me
and smiles as she gnaws

at my beautiful daughter who doesn't see
the old woman with curious grace
kiss her white throat
and unpeel her face

and my beautiful daughter grows very still,
thousands of miles, thousands of miles away,
and her tissued skin
fades into grey

and I see how the old woman hates
both me and my daughter
with hate thicker than blood
and stronger than water

and I call out in fear
to my beautiful daughter. Thin, grey and near
the old face shifts
and my daughter is here.

I am an old woman
and she is my daughter;
we are thousands of miles away
across much deep water.

WHEN MY DAUGHTER GOES DOWN TO THE DARK

Even before she goes, she stops eating.
We're up to the neck in harvest loaves
and melons and grapes and nectarines
and she sips, sips cold bottled water,
crumbles a morsel of empty toast,
touches her lips with a hollow spoon.

She knows, of course, his fondness for bone,
desire that flares for the concave pelvis,
lust for the shaft of shoulder and shin.
And she knows he will have no telephone.

Her eyes deepen. She puts on pearls,
dresses herself in darkest blue.
Shadows soften her mouth and chin;
new frost sparkles beneath her skin.

I hold her briefly in desperate arms,
flinch at the sharpness of her frame,
say—nothing. The hardness of parting
turns all words to leaves. In my garden
I long to keep her. She moves away.
No use, she says, this dependency.

I cut back dead wood. She, down there,
pares her hands to their lonely skill,
curves to the task of claw and tendon,
bends to the banquet of seven seeds.

But she'll come back. She always comes back.
Or so she says. There are arrows like buds
in the brown beech hedge. Skulls of bulbs
sulk in the ground. Yellow, the grass
but not quite dead.

My love, my darling, my only daughter—
all I see in the world is Winter.
I beg you to change the doom that's on us.

Listen. This business is simply a myth.
No Underworld beckons, no Hades, no Throne,
no call for you to be anyone's Queen.
If, flesh of my flesh, bone of my bone,
you can make your own story—
will you come home?

OBSERVED BY THE MOON

To those of you still on the earth, I say this:

Throughout your days you will search, but you may not find.
  Your readers are elsewhere.
They are drinking a glass of water alone
  Or falling in love
  Or walking together in thick, deep snow.

They will not be there when you want them or need them.
  They will turn to you and see nothing.
  They have their own preoccupations.

Nevertheless, their distant presence must steady you.
  When your words, meant solely for them, are praised by others—
  Do not attend.

Much is written and washed away.
Much is washed far away and lost.
  This is a clean and lonely space.

INSTRUMENT

You hear nervousness—yes
and no— a tremor—not
nervousness. It's just

the faith I am carrying.
Spirits of air and dust,
absent and present.

They have enormous trust
but they send such sadness
and all I have is my voice.

WHAT THIS POEM WILL NOT DO

end here. This is death but not ending. Make it easy. Few
repetitions and right turnings, therefore, but along the road
the small bodies of the crushed the bloodied the muddied and
feathered

my skin—look—the skin across the back of my hand is soft
and wrinkled. It is gentle. I have worn it a long time, put my
fingers to flex in it each morning, stretched, yawned, reached
for the keys. My eyes are green with glints of hazel. They have
seen life and death and forgotten both.

Baby, I know what I say but do you

think you are cool think you can drive this poem take it in one
swerve? Did you bring your whole self to the enterprise? I
think not. I can wind you in shred by red shred until you are
skinned. On every road sadness dazzles. Turn left. Left. You are
blind. I have killed. Come with me: we will travel together
through carnage and alas

you have missed much already. And I have missed only what
will not

THE MR AND MRS PHILPOTT POEMS

MR AND MRS PHILPOTT ON
HOLIDAY AT AUCHTERAWE

Mr Philpott, sitting naked in the conservatory,
examines the clouds descending on Ben Tee
in a distant squall. The sun sips at his skin
urging an instant pinkness. Mrs Philpott
(she is his second wife; he calls her 'dear')
bears in the morning beverage on a tray.
She is wearing a fresh apron, frilled with coy
rosebuds. Her lips open, enjoining him
to put on the Welsh Male Choirs—put them on *loud*.
Her wish is his command. Removing his glasses, he
flicks a switch which swells men's voices into
exultation, flooding the world with a surge
of joy. Outside the rain descends in sheets;
inside, the milk discreetly cools the tea.

On holiday without her children, Mrs Philpott
washes the towels and waits for them to dry.
Mr Philpott has gone up the burn with his rod
and his waders. What are they doing now,
her distant, grown-up babies? Taller than her
and wiser, they have told her there's no use
regretting the past: the prams, the pushchairs;
things, they say, move on, as people must—and she
should settle down, be positive, face it.
Therefore each week she lets herself unfold
a little curve of fat. *Voluptuous,*
as Mr Philpott calls it. Do you think, he says,
we're in love? I want only you, she replies, and sighs.
Truth approaches. She doesn't embrace it.

In the conservatory, Mr Philpott waits in the dark
with only the moon for company. They have had a row,
he and she, a marital discordancy, jangling of nerves.
Outside, the hills' grey curves and silver thighs
merge into softness, rain slipping slow and steady
as heartbeats. Inside, the silence swells and forms
a statement: *absence of love, absence of love.*
He absorbs the repetition, hearing her move
in the distant house, somewhere near but far. Packing,
maybe. Folding neat underwear, sheathing cool silk
in a calm green suitcase which travels well. He reaches
at last for the Welsh voices. Choral remedies—
can they suffice? Hands trembling, he pauses—
inserts the CD. Perhaps he may yet be saved.

Mr Philpott wakes in the blue bedroom. Beside him
Mrs Philpott dozes, her soft white shoulders curving
into dreams. Between the floral curtains, sun
spills from the conservatory, where saving
graces still are dancing. Sleepless, Philpott
counts his many losses. He has lost
his sons, his thin first wife, his confidence—
all of them gone. He turns to his cowrie shell
of safety, slipping one arm beneath her neck,
the other round her waist in the way she likes,
his skin breathing her in. Soon, he reflects,
there'll be toast and marmalade, the home-made, sweet-
bitter conserve of love. Ah George, she moans.
in her sleep. *George.* It is not his name.

George is not his name. But George isn't here—thus
Philpott consoles himself. Sadly he flies off
to sleep, airy and feathered. Mrs Philpott is dreaming
of pigs, a whole herd of them, and she's riding
the chief boar, clinging to yellow tusks. Spines cut
her inner thighs, searing the skin. Stop! she cries
but the ride goes harder, faster, until the brute
rears his huge head. It is George, her first husband:
he has got her now. Ah George, she pleads,
George—let me go. *No, no, by the hair on my
chinny chin chin,* he snaps, beard extended.
Almost too late, a white bird drops, enfolding her
in its wings. *You are voluptuous,* it sings. *Come.*
She embraces, weeping, the man who is holding her.

LEAVING

'I will leave you, George. I will go.'
Her voice always wavered.
Later she would pay.

'I shall go. One day you will wake.
I'll be gone.'
She said it too often.

The small birds in the garden
flew in and away.
She delayed.

Speedwell shimmered
in the blue lawn.
Her heart was long gone.

She went shopping
and found she had not returned.
It was done.

If she had only known
as she watched, watched the small birds go,
it would not be over

over over
the leaving in the Spring,
in the Winter leaving.

WIDOWED

Christmas is a bad time to die. Bad.
It wasn't as if she was old. Thin—
yes—but she'd always been thin, she didn't
approve of food. Unforgiving
and graceful and thin. Good with children,
fond of dogs, but distant to him.
So much between them had gone unsaid.

She would have been forty-nine in May. May
or might—this time he was on his own.
She just felt a pain, they did some kind of scan
and kept her in. She greyed to stone
in a week—and was gone. Neither son
could believe it. Reproachful, they frowned.
He should have known. What could he say?

He didn't know what to say, had never known.
If he brought flowers, she would ask why.
She had never let him see her cry.
She had never let him *see*. In some agony
of her own, she didn't let him in. He wouldn't pry.
They weren't the sort of people who are happy.
At her request, after the ceremony,
she was scattered as ash. Winnowed and blown.

So much between them had come untied.
Wife. Bride. Twenty-four years wed
and then laid to rest. In his head
he thought he was mad. He should have made
more of her, made more of love. But the funeral bed
was all full of ashes. If she had *said*—
if he had been less afraid—less terrified—
but it was done. After she died, he prayed.

AFTERWARDS

At the kitchen window,
in his dressing-gown,
Philpott stands alone
His sons have gone.
He's on his own.

His mouth draws a line
white as the frost
which furs the fence
and the garden shed.
The earth is hard.
The world's in bed.
No point in Christmas
when you are dead.

No point at all.
He stands as still
as bloodless stone,
unnoticed, he thinks,
by anyone—
but he is wrong.

On the roof-tops
starlings gather;
sparrows feather the birch
like leaves.
They watch him get
a knife to cut
the black-in-white,
the dark, sweet bread.

Philpott aches
for the Christmas cake,
the slice he took
for someone's sake
who isn't here.
How can he eat?
He has no heart—
just this—to break
at the cold front door.

Clumsy and numb,
he scatters outside
currant and crumb—

and the small birds come.

CLEANER

Mrs Philpott cleans the bathroom
cleaner than any living soul.

She scrubs the bath with a nylon brush,
steams the tiles with her steam machine,
sprays with anti-bacterial spray,
polishes with a spotless cloth

and sometimes as she cleans she sings
in a high clear voice that no-one hears
but the bathroom and its silent walls
and the mirror and the laundered towels
and the patient, gleaming toilet bowl.

If this hadn't been her special gift—
perhaps that day as she stood in the hall
unhooking her coat from the pegs to leave,
he wouldn't have noticed the gentle blush
dusting the inside curve of her arm;
he wouldn't have thought: it is like the rush
of light in the beech hedge when each hard bud,
surprised into softness, unfolds.

MONEY

It's never enough.
Philpott gets out his books and sighs.
All the time it is there, the burden of it,
money, money and only money.
Money on Monday and Tuesday and Wednesday,
money on Sunday
and the money files staring, cash and ledger,
share and stock, bond and yield,
red chips and blue.

His chair at the dining-room table is smooth.
The parquet floor shines,
the table-top gleams with bees-wax polish
but words in his head say
money, money and *never enough.*

In the garden, the green-gold leaves of nasturtiums
open their faces like coins to the sky
and one flower opens, blood-red.

Philpott's dead wife had life insurance.
She left much money in place of herself.
It's never enough.

Offshore funds, equities, gilts and derivatives,
futures and pasts.
There's a terrible cost, a terrible cost.
He scribbles a note in the blue column,
checks Friday's *Financial Times.*

His second wife puts a pheasant to roast
with thyme and chervil and rosemary,
then picks up her sewing: a tapestry,
a caravan of desert camels
making their way to an Arab tent.
She smiles at the thought of tent stitch for tents,
smiles and selects a mercerised strand.

Philpott feels something like despair
but drier and quieter.
He wants to stop counting.
He wants to enfold his lovely wife
and listen to life whispering in her thighs
and give up everything, save only this.

Mrs Philpott threads a camel
through the eye of her needle.

A HESITATION OVER SOCKS

Philpott has never hesitated over socks
until today. His hose lie ironed
in a special drawer, soles aired
in wool-rich patience, two by two
queued to be worn. On rising he always
surveys the ranks, sweeping his gaze
across grey and blue, worsted and plain,
awaiting the surge, the groin tingle,
the firm herald saluting his choice.

But today droops limp and uncertain.
No cock crow of confidence, rush of the blood.
He stares at the glass, seeing the briskness
drain from his face. Could he be ill?
A shuddered chill of Winter encroaches
as, safe in her kitchen, his wife announces
irrelevant breakfast. He slumps on the bed,

collapsed to a sigh—and nearly misses
the electrically obvious Royal Ramblers,
rich green footwear with feature toes,
a left foot and right foot, carefully hung
over the Dimplex in twinned content.
His manhood lifts and his heart with it.
Mrs Philpott has done it. She's laid them ready.
He pulls on his socks and his shoes and he walks
swiftly, smartly down every stair
to her unexpected self and kisses her.

PHILPOTT IN THE INSH MARSHES

Philpott, ensconsed in his hide, records all that he sees
in the Insh Marshes, wetland of wader and gull.
He notes down the purple thyme, the visiting bees
and one buzzard, which circles precisely and falls
down a seam of invisible air to a blur of grass.

Such an ache for the sky inhabits the portly watcher
peering, binoculared, at untrodden grounds.
He yearns for the spotted crake, for the dowitcher,
and would, if he could, ascend. But his speckled hands
are not wings, merely tools of an aging, forgetful teacher

who ought to go home. There's the fire to be laid,
wife to cajole. He is late. The newspaper nudges
its need to be read. There are meals to be paid for or made,
showers to fix. Meanwhile the different sedges,
all twenty-six, have ripened and planted sharp seeds

in his brain. At bedtime he fidgets, fusses and sighs,
thinking of sex and bills and owls, until
sleep takes him, dropping from artexed skies
to glean his hot body. His spotted pyjamas cool,
he loosens his grip on the quilted earth and flies

out through the window and up to a flood of stars.
He's done this before. With practised restraint, he lets
the currents of swirling night bear him slow and far
over the marshes where great pools of silence, velvet
and deep, await. He circles, skims birch-tops, plummets—

Alarmed, he descends to breakfast, smears lemon curd
on his toast, informs Mrs Philpott how osprey defend
the nest. She remarks, as so often before, how absurd
it is for a man of his age to spend every weekend
in a hut—like a hermit—and all just to look at some bird.

Mutely he fetches in logs, the fresh split timber
of last year's tree. He winnows soft ash to a pile,
puts kindling in criss-crossed sticks over sleeping embers,
then stalls, puzzled, somewhere halfway to a smile
as a spark flies. He can't quite—perhaps—remembers.

PRESERVES

The sweetness of June, a summons conveyed
from strawberry fields, calls her to pick.
She drives to the farm, the car arrayed

with Tupperware tubs. Always she takes
only the small fruits, sips first and last—
careful to check the magic she makes

is subtle and true. At home, the jars
are washed and waiting, parched for the swell
of slick thick lava reddened in glass.

July—and raspberries now compel
their ritual feast. Nothing can stop
the droop of canes, the crimson bells

burdened with seeds and desperate to drop
in her open palm. Slowly she lets
the red juice seep. In jam, the sleep

of Summer simmers, part of the heart
of the jam maker. She fires her pan
into melody and the music sets

rasps of ruby, sharp refrain
in a mildly-labelled, covered pot—
and the gentle house is calm again.

September. Brambles. Bold brash glut.
Black-mailed jelly. Bastard strain,
blood of the emperors, purple suit

potent as damson. This is no lean
harvest lament, no call to the weak
or lily-livered. The wild demesne

of danger beckons. Soon she will take
a stick to the hedge-rows, bustle and shove
and conquer thickets, no less for the sake

of bramble jelly than slow-trickled love
through muslined October and chill November
and then the bleaker days, the grave

memories that come with December
and long January, locked and still,
when each year she almost forgets to remember

the oranges—saviours from Seville,
the unlikely, lumpy friends. She ought to
make ready sooner. She runs to fill

her jam pan with oranges, covers with water
and heats. Listen. The whole house is made
safe with the song, the smell of laughter,

flood of light in a forest glade,
sweet-bitter sunset. Marmalade.

LIFE INSURANCE

The Insurance Man wants money.
He mentions the matter of 'peace of mind'.
Mrs Philpott, who rarely gets angry,
is tempted to give him a piece of her mind.

All the money in all the pots and all the pantries of the world
doesn't buy peace. Not one piece of peace.
It's one thing worrying about a fridge.
You can fix a fridge, you can get a new one.
There's no earthly policy known to man
which will compensate for a living person.

Of course, it may not come to that.
Mr Philpott scribbles a cheque.
The man relaxes and picks up his hat.

Mrs Philpott goes to take
a corn-fed chicken out of the freezer.
Later Mr Philpott sees her
in the kitchen, at the window
watching the trees, the way the wind blows,
the way the leaves fall fast and furious.

He stands very near her,
sees what she sees.
It is safer, closer.

CURTAINS

Once she slept in a pink room
with another husband and closed drapes
but now the walls are trickled with green,
rising in stripes to a corniced ceiling—
and Philpott prefers the curtains open.

In solemn ritual every night
he puts on his carefully ironed pyjamas,
steps to the window, opens the curtains,
peers at the night, sighs once or twice,
climbs into bed and falls asleep.

Sometimes she finds it hard to follow;
the white moon washes her laundered pillows;
his sleeping skin smells of new grass.
Sometimes she is possessed by lust;
sometimes by overwhelming loss. Outside

the luminous sky looks in. The stars are remote
and see too much. The wind insists
on being heard, and no muffling curtains
keep it out. Moonlight selects
the polished dresser, the silver hairbrush,

the photographs. Philpott's two sons, smiling
and thin; her unforgiving and angry daughters,
one on a skateboard; the children's dog.
Too dark to see, but all of them there
waiting, like her, for the Resurrection

when graves will open and all of the world
shall find itself in the promised frame:
man and first wife forever unsundered,
flesh of that flesh, bone of that bone
joined in the terrible sight of God

in the pink room with the pink curtains
which clamp for certain around her heart
like the shut shell of a dead oyster.
'Oyster?' says Philpott, his shrimping net
trawling the rocks and pools of dreams.

'Give me fresh sole. I never eat oysters.'
Hush, she soothes, hush my darling—
curving her warmth against his shoulder,
cradling his anxious meadow of skin,
facing the wide, uncurtained window.

LIGHT

His father died at fifty-eight
and so he will die at fifty-eight.
He fetches a tumbler.
Two years to go.

Soothed by Glenlivet
glittered on ice
he sits, he watches
the endless news:

wars and finance,
global warming,
olympic games,
lotteries churning.

His wife looks up
from her careful sewing.
Something about his face
is changing—

the lines round his eyes
are luminous;
a silver burnish
kisses his lips;

he is so still
that a kind of halo
spreading like grace
from inside the person

floods the room
and her hands with light.
She hardly knows
what to make of it.

THE VISITOR

Illness, leaning on a stick, stands by the fire.
No-one invited him.
None of the ceremonies are secure.
He is unguessed.
His eyes are intimate and familiar.
All his old friends are doctors.
His arms are numb. Dead embers.
Slowly he raises one blue finger.

There were only two people living here.
Now there are three.
Illness is related to marriage by despair.
He means to stay.
He means to unlock his black mouth and speak.
On the instant Philpott is awake.

He is awake and shivering in his bed which is like the sea,
a turmoil of waves and no shore
and his wife in the sheets, her glass eyes open,
sees too much in the dark, too far
and between them a thin, cold presence lies—
the silent body of the visitor.

ANGER

Philpott's anger lives in his shoes.
It tangles in the laces
and he wrestles like a lover

until it transforms
and he tries to hold on
but the battle is long.

First his dead wife,
whose fingers are strong,
enters the ring

and he struggles with her, struggles
till she turns back to anger
and leaves a new danger:

his tall son, first-born,
wiry fighter,
cursing his father

and there's no winning
the tugging and straining—
no owning, disowning

but only the noose, the noose of life
that suffocates
and won't be appeased

and the knots are fast,
their anger rolling
from sole to lace.

STOPPING

Mr Philpott is very tired. He would like to stop.

He would like time. He would like time to be careful and slow
like the man down the road who is trimming the lawn with
                                    kitchen scissors.
He would like to watch the sun on the carpet,
watch it travel from the wall to the chair by the door.
He would like to listen to the noises of the house,
to hear the hairs on his own arm stir.

Perhaps it is a sign. Ill people have to stop.
They stop and listen to the call of pain.
Perhaps it is coming and he had better move
quickly before it's too late, move quickly
before stopping happens. He has no pain
but this wanting to stop—it may be a sign.

Already he has keys in his hand, his leather briefcase
and his brisk face on. He has wasted an hour
and there's work to be done.

HEADACHE

Mrs Philpott pads secretly downstairs,
going by touch. Her fingers feel for the banister
in the rich dark. The carpet whispers

slow, slow. The house is peopled by creaks.
A line of grey is the kitchen door.
Slatted blinds slice up the night.

She strokes the big fridge. It purrs and hums.
Her headache demands: *Come on, come on.*
She pulls the door open. Loud light drums.

Milk. She needs milk to help her sleep
and small white pills for her jagged brain.
She gulps the liquid straight from the jug.

The fridge whines. She makes no response.
She has to get back, somehow, upstairs
over the slivers of silver pain.

In the big bed by the open window
Philpott snores under the stars.
She lifts the duvet and slips inside.

Her body is milk and dazzled moon.
She floods the pool of her sleeping self.
He dreams she's discovered a way to drown.

CAKE

Bake a cake for a visitor.
The baker is wearing a rose-bud apron.
Her hair and hands are dusted with flour.

Eggs are waiting beside the cooker;
the butter and sugar are beaten to foam;
the wooden spoon is charged with power.

This is a cake descended of cakes
born in small ovens for generations,
a cake of fragrance and careful making.

A hint of almond is for forgiveness;
the soft lemon curd is for contrition;
vanilla summons the shade of sweetness.

The crumb of the cake will be pale and warm;
the scent of the cake will be clear as dawn;
the shape of the cake a golden sun.

It will rise, like heaven, and then be gone.

HAIR

At night Mrs Philpott lets down her hair;
she takes out the clasps and her hair tumbles,
once copper, now silver, her hair ripples
and flickers her neck and her white shoulders.
She sits on the chair, sits and remembers
and brushes her hair, and brushes and brushes.

Her husband is watching. Not looking, but watching
the shine on her hair, on her hair and her throat
and the strong strokes of her hand brushing,
the calm edge of her elbow turning,
the shadows that dimple her arm moving,
the clean sheen of her skin glistening

and the light on her hair in the room rushing
is like the spirit of water spilling
and falling over her living shoulders
and filling the air and the deep mirror
and bringing this man to an inner trembling
which nothing before in his life has ushered.

Perhaps he will gather this feeling in armfuls
and give it again to the woman waiting
with awe in her eyes and barely breathing
and hair, once copper, now silver glittering,
paused at last, and wondering, fearing,
hand on the hair brush poised and shivering—